HOW TO SMELL A FART

Radical Acceptance For Humans With Stinky Emotions.

Angelica Shiels Psy.D.

For all the adults who are searching for their inner child
and all the children who need their adults to find them.

This is a book about feelings that stink.

sometimes it comes out of nowhere.

It makes everything stinky.

The yucky part passed.

Hello there, old friend.
This feeling is just a feeling. It's elecrticity in my nerves. It doesn't mean I'm defective. It doesn't mean endless ick.
i accept this.
It's back.

50

"Radical acceptance" is a habit that helps people regulate their emotions. To "radically" accept something is to willingly accept that it exists *even when you don't like it.* It includes two steps:

1) Committing in your mind to willingly take- in all the feelings and realities the moment brings with it.
2) Surrendering your body to the physical sensations that the emotions of the moment bring.

Radical acceptance is applied to unchangeable things, specifically the unchangeable reality that exists *in the current moment.*

The current reality, including the emotional experiences in the moment, are unchangeable; they already DO exist. Exerting energy trying to resist the current moment is not just unproductive, but further dysregulates intense emotions.

Only when the current reality is accepted can a person make clear-minded change or constructively communicate (if that's what the situation calls for). Usually when people are resisting the current moment, they do and say things that make the current moment lead to a *worse* moment. When people *accept* the current reality, this creates space for the next moment to be intentional and *improved* if need-be.

When trying to "radically accept" the moment, remind yourself:
- It is possible to accept this reality even if I don't like it.
- There is a reason this reality exists as it exists, and I don't have to understand the reason in order to accept it.
- This moment is worth living, even though this reality exists as it does.

These are the contexts in which to especially practice radical acceptance:
- Initial emotions (uncontrollable. You can only intentionally add thoughts, sensations, and behaviors that indirectly alter emotions.)
- Initial thoughts (uncontrollable. You can only control what you add to your thoughts/focus-on intentionally.)
- The aspects and qualities of the moment you're IN.

The best gift that you can give yourself, your spouse, and your children, is to practice radically accepting emotions and moments as they are.

Adult reader, does a little stinker inside you need you to accept their feeling in a moment?

Made in the USA
Las Vegas, NV
10 April 2024

88497854R00036